Pray your way through!

Always make time to spend with God.

Girl you've got this!

Make your prayer life a Lifestyle!

Cry out to God he is always waiting to hear

from us..

I love you and I'm praying that your

situation changes.

This Prayer Journal belongs to:

_____

Date received:

_____

Hey God, I want to give up but,

2 Chronicles 15:7

_____

_____

_____

_____

_____

_____

_____

_____

_____

_____

_____

_____

_____

_____

_____

_____

_____

_____

_____

Hey God, I'm tired but,
Psalm 4:8

Hey God, I'm stressed out but,

Isaiah 41:10

_____

_____

_____

_____

_____

_____

_____

_____

_____

_____

_____

_____

_____

_____

_____

_____

_____

_____

_____

Hey God, I'm broken but,
Psalm 147:3

_____

_____

_____

_____

_____

_____

_____

_____

_____

_____

_____

_____

_____

_____

_____

_____

_____

_____

_____

_____

Hey God, my rent is due but,

Isaih 41:10

_____
_____
_____
_____
_____
_____
_____
_____
_____
_____
_____
_____
_____
_____
_____
_____
_____
_____
_____
_____

Hey God,anxiety is kicking in but,

1Peter 5:7

Hey God, I got fired but,

Proverbs 19:11

_____
_____
_____
_____
_____
_____
_____
_____
_____
_____
_____
_____
_____
_____
_____
_____
_____
_____
_____
_____
_____
_____
_____

Hey God, I don't feel loved but,

John 3:16

_____

_____

_____

_____

_____

_____

_____

_____

_____

_____

_____

_____

_____

_____

_____

_____

_____

Hey God, depression is kicking in but,

Deuternomy 31:8

Hey God, I feel like I'm losing my mind but,

Jeremiaah 29:11

_____

_____

_____

_____

_____

_____

_____

_____

_____

_____

_____

_____

_____

_____

_____

_____

_____

_____

_____

_____

Hey God, I want more in life but,

Psalm 37:4

_____

_____

_____

_____

_____

_____

_____

_____

_____

_____

_____

_____

_____

_____

_____

_____

_____

_____

_____

_____

Hey God, I feel helpless but,

Psalm 121:1

Hey God, my mind is restless but,

Proverbs 15:16

_____
_____
_____
_____
_____
_____
_____
_____
_____
_____
_____
_____
_____
_____
_____
_____
_____
_____
_____
_____
_____

Hey God, I'm going through a bad breakup but,

Psalm 34:18

_____

_____

_____

_____

_____

_____

_____

_____

_____

_____

_____

_____

_____

_____

_____

_____

_____

_____

Hey God, my husband don't love me but,

1Corinthians 7:3-5

_____

_____

_____

_____

_____

_____

_____

_____

_____

_____

_____

_____

_____

_____

_____

_____

_____

_____

_____

Hey God, my children don't obey me but,

Ephesians 6:1

_____

_____

_____

_____

_____

_____

_____

_____

_____

_____

_____

_____

_____

_____

_____

_____

_____

_____

Hey God, I'm facing eviction but,

Leviticus 20:22

Hey God, no food in my house but,

Psalm 146:6-7

_____

_____

_____

_____

_____

_____

_____

_____

_____

_____

_____

_____

_____

_____

_____

_____

_____

_____

Hey God, I'm addicted to porn but,

Corinthians 10:13

_____

_____

_____

_____

_____

_____

_____

_____

_____

_____

_____

_____

_____

_____

_____

_____

_____

_____

_____

_____

_____

Hey God, I feel helpless but,
Isaiah 12:2

_____

_____

_____

_____

_____

_____

_____

_____

_____

_____

_____

_____

_____

_____

_____

_____

_____

_____

Hey God, I'm lost in this world but,

Deuteronomy 31:8

Hey God, I want to be fully commited to you but,

James 4:8

_____

_____

_____

_____

_____

_____

_____

_____

_____

_____

_____

_____

_____

_____

_____

_____

_____

_____

Hey God, I want to start my business but,

Habakkuk 2:2

_____

_____

_____

_____

_____

_____

_____

_____

_____

_____

_____

_____

_____

_____

_____

_____

_____

Hey God, feels like nothing is going right but,

Proverbs 3:5-6

_____

_____

_____

_____

_____

_____

_____

_____

_____

_____

_____

_____

_____

_____

_____

_____

_____

_____

_____

Hey God, I want to love wholeheartedly but,

John 15:12-13

_____

_____

_____

_____

_____

_____

_____

_____

_____

_____

_____

_____

_____

_____

_____

_____

_____

_____

_____

_____

Hey God, the doctors gave me a diagnose but,

Hebrews 11:1

Hey God, the devil is playing with my mind but,

1Corinthians 2:16

Hey God, I want to enjoy life but,

Matthew 6:19

Hey God, I want to give my children the world but,

Psalm 127:3-5

_____

_____

_____

_____

_____

_____

_____

_____

_____

_____

_____

_____

_____

_____

_____

_____

_____

_____

Hey God, my business is slow but,

Philippians 1:6

_____

_____

_____

_____

_____

_____

_____

_____

_____

_____

_____

_____

_____

_____

_____

_____

_____

_____

Hey God, my tuition is due but,
Proverbs 14:23

_____

_____

_____

_____

_____

_____

_____

_____

_____

_____

_____

_____

_____

_____

_____

_____

_____

_____

_____

Hey God, I'm serving you in church but,

Hebrews 4:13

_____

_____

_____

_____

_____

_____

_____

_____

_____

_____

_____

_____

_____

_____

_____

_____

_____

_____

_____

_____

Hey God, I want to write a book but,

Jeremiah 30:2

Hey God, I've been rejected so many times but,

Romans 8:28

Hey God, my light is off but,
1Peter 3:14

_____

_____

_____

_____

_____

_____

_____

_____

_____

_____

_____

_____

_____

_____

_____

_____

_____

_____

_____

Hey God, I want to pray more but,

Matthew 6:33

_____

_____

_____

_____

_____

_____

_____

_____

_____

_____

_____

_____

_____

_____

_____

_____

_____

_____

_____

_____

Hey God, I want to study your word more but,

Psalm 4:1

_____

_____

_____

_____

_____

_____

_____

_____

_____

_____

_____

_____

_____

_____

_____

_____

_____

Hey God, I want to relocate but,

Proverbs 16:3

_____

_____

_____

_____

_____

_____

_____

_____

_____

_____

_____

_____

_____

_____

_____

_____

_____

Hey God, I wan't to give up but,
2 Chronicles 15:7